# KOMODO DRAGONS

LIVING WILD

## LIVING WILD

Published by Creative Paperbacks
P.O. Box 227, Mankato, Minnesota 56002
Creative Paperbacks is an imprint of The Creative Company
www.thecreativecompany.us

Design and production by Mary Herrmann
Art direction by Rita Marshall
Printed by Corporate Graphics in the United States of America

Photographs by 123RF (Steve Estvanik, Kira Kaplinski), Alamy (A&J Visage, Reinhard Dirscherl, Mark Eveleigh, M@rcel, Ville Palonen, Travel Ink), Corbis (Naturfoto Honal, Phil Noble/Reuters), Dreamstime (Bobonacus, Mark Eastment, Michael Elliott, Steve Estvanik, Fonetix, Mark Higgins, Iorboaz, Ruslan Kokarev, Zune Shing Lim, Pebat, Pniesen, Webitect, Henry Wong), Getty Images (Buyenlarge/Time & Life Pictures, Fox Photos, Straits Times/AFP, Michele Westmorland), iStockphoto (Rob Broek, Christine Glade, Rudy Suryana Sentosa, Anna Yu)

Copyright © 2012 Creative Paperbacks
International copyright reserved in all countries. No part of this book may be reproduced in any form without written permission from the publisher.

The Library of Congress has cataloged the hardcover edition as follows:
Gish, Melissa.
Komodo dragons / by Melissa Gish.
p. cm. — (Living wild)
Includes bibliographical references and index.
Summary: A look at Komodo dragons, including their habitats, physical characteristics such as their sawlike teeth, behaviors, relationships with humans, and threatened status in the world today.
ISBN 978-1-60818-080-6 (hardcover)
ISBN 978-0-89812-672-3 (pbk)
1. Komodo dragon—Juvenile literature. I. Title.

QL666.L29G49 2011
597.95'968—dc22     2010028307

CPSIA: 110310 PO1385

9 8 7 6 5 4 3 2

# KOMODO DRAGONS
Melissa Gish

A warm breeze blows across
the hills of Komodo Island,

ruffling the grassy hiding spot of a Komodo dragon.

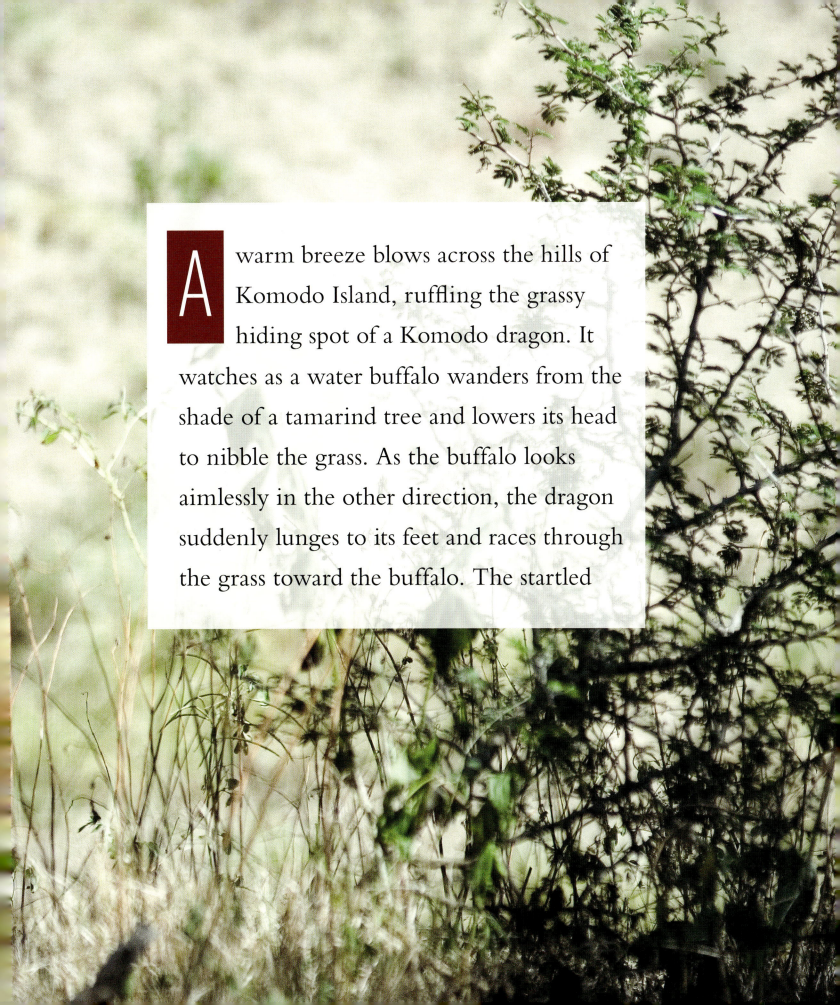

A warm breeze blows across the hills of Komodo Island, ruffling the grassy hiding spot of a Komodo dragon. It watches as a water buffalo wanders from the shade of a tamarind tree and lowers its head to nibble the grass. As the buffalo looks aimlessly in the other direction, the dragon suddenly lunges to its feet and races through the grass toward the buffalo. The startled buffalo's legs bend as it turns to flee—but it cannot move quickly enough. The dragon bites the buffalo's hind leg and then dashes away. Grunting, the buffalo disappears into the forest. But the dragon has not lost its prize. The toxins in its bite will lead to deadly blood loss and infection. In a week the buffalo will be dead, and its killer will track it to its final resting place, where the dragon will enjoy a feast.

## WHERE IN THE WORLD THEY LIVE

■ **Komodo Dragon**
Indonesia

The single species of Komodo dragon is found primarily on the Indonesian islands of Komodo and Rinca. A limited number also live nearby on Flores and Gili Motang. The colored square represents the dragons' restricted range in the wild.

10    LIVING WILD

## KILLER LIZARDS

Unlike most large reptiles, which have changed little since the days of the dinosaurs, the Komodo dragon is a relatively new arrival on Earth. Smaller than its prehistoric ancestors, the Komodo dragon, the heaviest of all lizards, is an isolated species. Also called the Komodo monitor, this animal is found only on the Indonesian islands of Komodo, Flores, Gili Motang, and Rinca—located north of Australia between the Indian and Pacific oceans. First documented in 1910 on Komodo Island by Dutch **colonists**, Komodo dragons became exotic additions to zoos in the early 1900s. Mysterious and difficult to manage, Komodo dragons always perished quickly in captivity. These unique animals remained a mystery to science until recently. Only in the last 30 years have scientists unlocked many of the Komodo dragon's secrets.

The Komodo dragon, whose scientific name is *Varanus komodoensis*, is most closely related to the other venomous lizards in the Varanidae family. This group includes more than 50 species of monitor lizard, such as water monitors, emerald tree monitors, and the rare crocodile monitors of

*New Guinea's emerald tree monitor is only about a third the length of a mature Komodo dragon.*

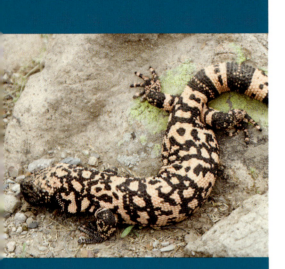

*Gila monsters have a venomous bite, but the slow-moving lizards have not caused a human death in recorded history.*

New Guinea. Komodo dragons' next-closest relatives are the two species of beaded lizard, the endangered beaded lizard of Guatemala and the Gila (*HEE-lah*) monster of the southwestern United States and northern Mexico.

Komodo dragons, called *oras* by the people of Indonesia, are reptiles. Reptiles are ectothermic animals, which means that their body temperature changes with the environment. When a Komodo dragon's body temperature gets too low, it must warm itself in the sun. When its body temperature gets too high, it must cool itself in shade or water. While most reptiles move slowly to conserve energy and body warmth, an attacking Komodo dragon can move swiftly and with great ferocity. Most reptiles, including Komodo dragons, reproduce by laying eggs.

To make up for their poor sense of smell and relatively few taste buds, dragons hunt using a combination of taste and smell. The dragon's specialized forked tongue gathers chemicals from the air and surrounding objects and then rubs them onto pads on the bottom of the mouth. The pads send signals to a special part of its nasal system called a Jacobson's organ, which translates the signals and sends messages to the brain. By analyzing chemicals in the air

*A dragon's tongue, which can be up to 16 inches (40.6 cm) long, allows it to "taste" the air and detect smells.*

*Because a dragon's gums cover its one-inch (2.5 cm) teeth, the lizard appears toothless—until it starts to bite.*

this way, dragons can "taste" **carrion** up to three miles (4.8 km) away.

Full-grown Komodo dragons average 150 pounds (68 kg) and measure 8 feet (2.4 m) long, though they have been known to reach 300 pounds (136 kg) and 10 feet (3 m) in length. The Komodo dragon is an apex predator in its island habitat—a mature dragon has no natural enemies. Its muscular body is completely covered by hard, protective scales. Each scale is connected by a nerve to a sensory plaque, a tiny organ that allows the dragon to feel things. Scales on the facial area and the soles of the feet have three or more sensory plaques apiece, which allow dragons more sensitivity when exploring the environment.

Komodo dragons have 60 flat, sawlike teeth that deliver deep wounds to prey animals such as deer and water buffalo, which can be as much as 5 times larger than the dragon. In addition, glands in the dragon's mouth release a venom that causes the bite wound to continuously bleed, and anything that is bitten by a Komodo dragon will usually die a slow, agonizing death. The trail of blood left by the animal enables the dragon

**Scientists have discovered that the Komodo dragon's bite is weaker but much deeper and therefore more damaging than a crocodile's.**

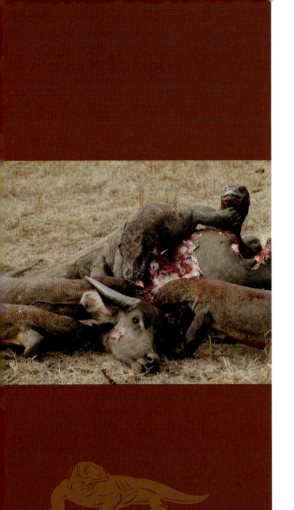

When Komodo dragons feast together on carcasses, a feeding frenzy similar to that of sharks ensues.

to track it. Because the bacteria in a Komodo dragon's mouth is more powerful than the bacteria found in rotting meat, the Komodo dragon is able to eat carrion without making itself sick.

Using its teeth like knife blades, the dragon saws off chunks of meat from a **carcass**. As a dragon bites down, its gums, which almost completely cover its teeth, tear and begin to bleed. The blood mixes with the dragon's saliva and creates a sort of slime that helps the dragon swallow food whole without chewing. Komodo dragons devour every part of a prey animal—feathers, fur, teeth, and even hooves—which are dissolved by the dragon's powerful stomach acids.

Komodo dragons hunt by ambushing their prey. **Camouflaged** by its drab coloration on a sandy shore or hidden in tall grass, a dragon will stay motionless for long periods of time, waiting for prey to come close enough to be bitten by a sudden strike. Komodo dragons have muscular legs and can chase prey at speeds of up to 13 miles (21 km) per hour for short bursts. However, running and breathing at the same time is difficult for reptiles, as they do not have the chest muscles necessary

for respiration. For this reason, the Komodo dragon developed a bony pouch in the throat called a gular pouch. This pouch is filled with air, which is pumped into the lungs, allowing dragons to sprint for short distances without breathing. Komodo dragons cannot lap or suck

*Komodo dragons are not the only creatures to sport a gular pouch; pelicans and their relatives also feature this unusual physical trait.*

A nictitating (NIK-tih-tayt-ing) membrane—a see-through inner eyelid—protects the Komodo dragon's eyes whenever it is active.

water like most animals, either. To drink, a Komodo dragon scoops up a mouthful of water, then tilts its head back to let the water flow down its throat.

Komodo dragons have five toes with sharp claws on each foot. Dragons use their front claws to hold prey to the ground or rip fur away from meat. Female dragons use their claws to dig nest chambers into which they can lay their eggs. Komodo dragons have eyelids that close to protect the eyes and ear openings on each side of the head that are covered by a thin flap of skin.

Komodo dragons can hear only those sounds limited to a range of low pitches. But because Komodo dragons rarely respond to sound, it was long thought that these animals were deaf. This theory was disproved in the 1990s when a keeper employed by the London Zoo trained a Komodo dragon to respond to the sound of her voice. Even when the dragon could not see its keeper, it reacted to her voice by going to its feeding station, where it apparently knew its keeper would feed it. Since this discovery, more research has been done to show that Komodo dragons can even differentiate between the voices of different people.

*The thick, fearsome claws of a Komodo dragon can grow to be two to three inches (5–7.6 cm) in length.*

*Creatures that obtain warmth or coolness from their environments are called poikilothermic (POY-ki-luh-THER-mik).*

## ISLAND GIANTS

On a typical day, a Komodo dragon may look more like a stone statue than a living creature. The dragons are inactive most of the time. They have a very slow **metabolism** and can go long periods of time without any water—up to nine months for adults. In order to **thermoregulate** their bodies, Komodo dragons spend cool mornings and evenings basking in the sun and hot days hidden in burrows, underneath trees, or soaking in watering holes—all the time waiting for prey to come close enough to grab.

Sambar deer and water buffalo are favorite large meals. One or the other is usually consumed about once a month. A Komodo dragon can eat about 80 percent of its body weight in a single meal. After consuming a deer or water buffalo, a Komodo dragon may need to sleep for up to a week while the food digests. Smaller snacks between meals may include snakes, lizards, birds, and rodents.

The dragons will feed on almost anything nearby—small and large **mammals**, birds, and even humans. Most deadly encounters with Komodo dragons occur

**Scientists believe that Komodo dragons can see in color and may even take special interest in objects that are red.**

**Up until 2009, scientists believed that bacterial infection, not venom, was responsible for the slow deaths of Komodo dragons' victims.**

in grassy areas, where dragons lie in wait for prey. Komodo dragons are even cannibalistic, meaning they will eat their own kind. Adult dragons commonly feed on younger, smaller dragons. They will kill dragon hatchlings as well as old or injured dragons that cannot defend themselves.

Komodo dragons are solitary animals for most of the year. Outside of mating season, they typically come together only to feed on a large carcass. Because males are larger than females and juveniles, they usually win fights over the biggest portions of meat, forcing the weaker dragons to seek food elsewhere. Male Komodo dragons live in separate territories, which they patrol daily and guard fiercely. Females and juveniles also inhabit these territories, but the only time a male Komodo dragon will allow another male to pass through his territory is while the visitor is tracking prey.

Left undisturbed, a Komodo dragon may live up to 50 years in the wild. The dragons mature at about six years of age, at which time they may begin breeding. Mating season is from May to August, and males fight for the right to court females. Two males will stand up

*When a male dragon rubs a female's chin, she flicks her tongue at him; if she does not like his taste, she runs away.*

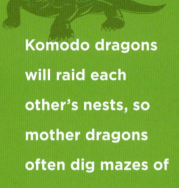

**Komodo dragons will raid each other's nests, so mother dragons often dig mazes of false tunnels to try to confuse egg raiders.**

on their hind legs, balanced on their tails like kangaroos, and wrestle with each other, trying to push each other to the ground. These matches can go on for long periods of time, with the weaker male eventually being pushed to the ground, sometimes landing in a twisted heap of broken legs or with its shoulders dislocated.

After the battle, the loser will lie still and allow the winner to scrape his claws along the loser's back and tail as a sign of dominance. Then the loser limps away, leaving the winner to approach the female. If a female is receptive, the male will rub his chin against her neck and back and nudge her with his nose. The female will not mate unless the male is strong enough to pin her down and hold her in place.

Not all Komodo dragons need to mate in order to reproduce, though. Some types of lizards and snakes are able to reproduce parthenogenically, which means that females can have babies without mating with males. In 2006, a Komodo dragon at London's Chester Zoo demonstrated that these animals are also capable of parthenogenesis when she produced eight offspring without having had any contact with a male Komodo dragon.

When a male and female do mate, each returns to its territory afterward. It takes four to five weeks after mating for the eggs to develop inside the female, during which time she digs a burrow in a warm location. Then she lays 10 to 30 eggs in her nesting burrow. Older females lay more eggs than younger ones do. The eggs are about the size of a baseball and feel like water balloons, but they are sturdy. The female covers them with dirt and vegetation to keep them warm. Then she guards her nest constantly for up to three months. By January (at the latest), the female can leave her nest unattended, as the risk of her eggs being disturbed is diminished by the onset of the rainy season. In April, when the months of almost continuous rain have come to an end and the forest has dried, the young Komodo dragons hatch.

A baby Komodo dragon uses its **egg tooth** to rip through the leathery shell of its egg. Hatchlings are only about 14 inches (35.6 cm) long at birth. They are greenish-gray with whitish-yellow stripes. As soon as they emerge from the nest, the hatchlings must dash to the trees, where their coloring provides

*Slender and flexible, young Komodo dragons can quickly attack smaller lizards in their treetop habitats.*

In 2003, the Toronto Zoo's captive-breeding program produced the first Komodo dragon hatched in Canada.

camouflage. Many do not make it, falling prey to birds, snakes, and other Komodo dragons—sometimes even their own mothers.

Those hatchlings that do reach the trees must spend the first four or five years of their lives as high off the ground as possible to avoid being eaten. In the trees, young Komodo dragons feed mainly on insects, eggs, and small birds. They develop quickly, growing 12 inches (30.5 cm) or more per year for about the first 4 years of their lives. When young dragons do come to the ground, often to find water, they must be cautious and swift.

When they reach about four feet (1.2 m) in length, Komodo dragons must come down from the trees permanently, as their weight can no longer be supported. By its fifth year, a Komodo dragon may be six feet (1.8 m) in length, and, unless it becomes sick or injured, it will have the strength to defend its territory against most potential threats, except older, much larger dragons. In one more year, the Komodo dragon will be fully mature and ready to rival other adults for feeding and breeding. It will continue to grow—though much more slowly—throughout its lifetime.

*Juvenile dragons are most at risk from their own kind, as they make up about 10 percent of an adult dragon's diet.*

## FROM *BEOWULF*

Then the monster began to spew forth coals of fire and burn the bright dwellings; the surging flame leaped forth, terrifying the people; the loathed flier of the air meant to leave naught in that place alive. The warfare of the dragon, the vengeance of the deadly foe, near and far was manifest, how the destroyer hated and humbled the Geatish folk. Ere break of day he shot back to his hoard again, to his dark and secret hall. He had encompassed the men of that land with flame, with fire and burning, trusting for defence in his mound, his wall, and his might in warfare;—his trust betrayed him!

And forthwith the terror was made known unto Beowulf, how for a truth his own home, best of halls, the gift-seat of the Geats, had melted away in waves of fire. . . . The fire-dragon with his burning coals had utterly destroyed the fortress, stronghold of the people, the water-washed fastness. Therefore the war-king, chief of the Weders, devised revenge upon him. Then the defence of warriors, lord of heroes, bade them make him a wondrous battle-shield, all of iron; for he knew full well that a shield of linden wood from the forest could avail him naught against the flame. But the valiant prince was doomed to meet the end of his fleeting days, of this worldly life, and the dragon too, though he had long held the hoarded treasure.

*Translated by C. B. Tinker (1902)*

## HERE BE DRAGONS

*The Hunt-Lenox Globe, named for former owners, is the only globe or map still in existence to display the famous Latin words.*

Dragons are **mythical** reptilian beasts with scales, sharp claws and teeth, and sometimes bearing wings. One of the first European stories, *Beowulf*, written between the 8th and 11th centuries, set the standard for dragons, depicting the creature as a deadly, fire-breathing monster. The second-oldest known globe, made in Europe about 1507, contained the first documented use of the Latin words *hic sunt dracones*, or "here be dragons." The words appeared in the area of coastal Southeast Asia. It then became a tradition for mapmakers to draw pictures of serpentlike sea creatures in blank areas of maps to signal that such parts of the world were unexplored and potentially dangerous. But in the East, many Asian traditions thought of dragons as symbols of good fortune and even used them to represent the Chinese emperors.

There are no real dragons, of course, but Komodo monitor lizards, as they are properly called, earned their common name from their aggressive behavior and yellow forked tongue—traits shared with the dragons of European legends. The name "monitor," from the Latin

**Young Komodo dragons may roll in feces to mask their odor and avoid becoming snacks for adult Komodo dragons.**

*monere*, meaning "to warn," was given to this group of lizards for a very different reason. In the 15th century, explorers such as Italian Niccolò de' Conti, who visited Malaysia and other parts of Southeast Asia in about 1421, believed that the large lizards they encountered stood up on their hind legs to monitor, or watch for, crocodiles. While monitor lizards do become agitated around crocodiles, there is no scientific proof that these lizards consciously give warning to others by observing crocodiles; nonetheless, the name was adopted.

In 1926, hunter-adventurer W. Douglas Burden was commissioned by New York's American Museum of Natural History to travel to the island of Komodo to investigate the strange creatures reported to live there. The story of Burden's expedition—whose members included a fellow big-game hunter, a **herpetologist**, and Burden's wife—became a legend as strange and exciting as the Komodo dragons themselves.

Burden tracked the lizards using their enormous footprints, then set baited traps for them. He was intent on shooting some as specimens to be stuffed at the museum and hoped to capture a live pair for a zoo

*A preserved dragon displayed at the London Zoo in the 1930s sparked the imaginations of spectators.*

exhibit. While assisting her husband, Mrs. Burden was charged by a dragon and nearly lost her life, but one of her companions shot it before it reached her. One particularly large dragon broke one of Burden's traps and struggled with Burden and his team for hours before it was finally contained in a cage made of heavy timber and steel mesh. The next morning, Burden found the cage torn apart and the dragon gone. The stories he had heard about the Komodo dragons—stories describing them as fierce creatures that frustrated even the most skilled trappers—appeared to be true.

KOMODO DRAGONS 31

*Park rangers carry long poles with forked ends that are used to poke dragons in the nose if they get too close.*

Ultimately, Burden returned to New York with 12 dead specimens for the museum and 2 live Komodo dragons, which he sold to the Bronx Zoo. Burden also recounted the story of his trip to movie producer Merian C. Cooper—the man who would use Burden's tale, swapping a giant ape in place of a giant lizard, as the inspiration for his 1933 film *King Kong*.

A Komodo dragon is the centerpiece of the 1990 film *The Freshman*, which stars Matthew Broderick as a college student enlisted to illegally deliver a Komodo dragon to a secret restaurant known for putting rare and endangered species on its menu. But because Komodo dragons do not respond well to handling, no actual dragons appear in the film. An Asian water monitor, which most closely resembles the Komodo dragon, was used in its place. The 1999 film *Komodo* also stars Komodo dragons—but in name only, yet again. Set on a remote island where dragons are the subject of secret scientific experiments, the film features computer-generated images of gigantic Komodo dragons that gruesomely chomp anything—or anyone—they can grab.

While real-life Komodo dragon attacks on people are rare, the native peoples of Komodo and Rinca have a realistic

*When Merian C. Cooper wrote King Kong, he originally wanted Kong to battle a group of Komodo dragons.*

*The sole, small village on Komodo Island is supported by the fishing and tourism industries.*

fear of the dragons. They do not approach the dragons or antagonize them, and they warn tourists to never walk into the forest or grasslands alone. A long-held belief in a special relationship they shared with the dragons has—up until very recently—resulted in people keeping a respectful distance between themselves and the dragons. For many generations, Komodo Islanders would feed old dragons that could no longer hunt, throwing out deer heads and hides and fish heads and guts to the dragons that lived nearby. Younger dragons would sometimes join in the feast as well. The islanders believed this peace offering was what kept them and their children safe from attack.

This seemed to be the case, as only 1 human death caused by a Komodo dragon had been documented in Indonesia in the 30 years since records were first kept in 1965. In 1995, Komodo Island park authorities banned the feeding of wild Komodo dragons and outlawed dogs—considered an invasive species—on the island. Dogs had traditionally been used to keep dragons out of villages. Environmentalists supporting the bans felt that feeding the dragons could result in the dragons' growing lazy and forgetting how to hunt for themselves. Villagers argued that by not continuing the tradition of feeding the dragons and by eliminating the dogs that had kept the dragons at bay, people would become vulnerable to dragon attacks. Indeed, Komodo dragons have killed several people since 2000, and villagers live in fear of **nuisance** dragons that have recently begun to freely enter school buildings and homes.

Because Komodo dragons have such a fierce reputation, they are popular features on wildlife television shows such as Animal Planet's *The Crocodile Hunter*, *Corwin's Quest*, *Up Close and Dangerous*, *Raw Nature*, and *The Most Extreme*, one of the cable station's longest-running documentary series, which named the Komodo dragon the third-most extreme biter—after the cookie cutter shark and the hippopotamus. Brothers Chris and Martin Kratt took viewers of their National Geographic Channel series *Be the Creature* on a trip to Komodo Island, and the late Steve Irwin, better known as the Crocodile Hunter, included Komodo dragons in his 1999 video, *The Crocodile Hunter: Steve's Most Dangerous Adventures*. Viewers can see just how fast Komodo dragons move as they chase Irwin up a tree—displaying why they are the kings of their habitats.

*People entering the forest to harvest fruit do so armed against possible encounters with hungry dragons.*

**Komodo National Park estimates the human population within parkland has increased 800 percent over the last 60 years.**

KOMODO DRAGONS 35

*Since the fossil age, nearly 9,000 species of reptiles have evolved to exist today; about 3,800 of them are lizards.*

NATIONAL TREASURES

While reptiles were well established on Earth 300 million years ago, the first monitor lizards **evolved** only about 40 million years ago in Asia. They spread to Australia about 15 million years ago when Australia's landmass collided with Southeast Asia. Lower sea levels that occurred about two million years later allowed the lizards to travel between islands that had formed, and they evolved into a variety of species.

At that time, large mammals such as dwarf elephants existed on the islands and were likely prey for the lizards, which steadily grew bigger. The largest ancestor of the Komodo dragon, the enormous *Megalania prisca*, grew to more than 23 feet (7 m) in length and 1,400 pounds (635 kg) in weight, making it the largest venomous animal to have ever lived. Dwarf elephants went **extinct** 25,000 years ago, and the dragons gradually reduced in size again. About 10,000 years ago, sea levels rose, and Komodo dragons became isolated on the islands on which they are found today.

Much of the public's attention focuses on endangered species that are cute and cuddly—pandas and polar bears,

*Scientists speculate that a massive volcanic eruption caused the dwarf elephants of Indonesia to die out.*

KOMODO DRAGONS 37

**When a wildfire destroyed Padar Island in 1984, Komodo dragons swam to other islands, leaving Padar now empty of dragons.**

for example. But other species—some that are not cute, are definitely not cuddly, and are often downright mean—are also at risk of extinction and need to be recognized as creatures worth saving. The Komodo dragon is one such species. While the current population of about 5,000 dragons is considered stable, only about 350 of these are breeding females. This may be enough to sustain the population for the time being, but scientists and conservationists wonder how long Komodo dragons will remain safe.

Although most native people living near Komodo dragon habitats respect the dragons and work to protect them, Komodo dragons are not invulnerable to human interference. Because the islands on which Komodo dragons live are small and isolated, the expansion of cities into dragon habitats may leave dragons with smaller territories and less available prey. **Poaching** is also a major threat to Komodo dragons, which may be killed for their skins and feet. And young dragons are illegally captured for sale to private collectors of exotic animals.

Natural disasters are another cause for concern. While there are no active volcanoes on the islands where

Komodo dragons live, nearby islands contain active and semi-active volcanoes and are also prone to earthquakes. The underwater volcano Gili Banta, Komodo Island's nearest volcanic neighbor at just over 6 miles (9.7 km) away, has not erupted since 1957, but Sangeang Api, or Fire Mountain, located 31 miles (50 km) northwest of Komodo Island, last erupted in 1997. Such recent activity has led scientists to theorize that one major volcanic eruption or one major earthquake on any of the nearby islands or underwater in the vicinity of dragon habitats could trigger a massive tidal wave that would strike Komodo, Flores, Gili Motang, and Rinca, potentially decimating the Komodo dragon populations.

Determining the level of conservation that Komodo

*Komodo National Park protects dragons and other wildlife and includes the islands of Komodo, Rinca, and Padar.*

*A traditional Asian healing art called acupuncture has successfully treated sick dragons at the Singapore Zoo.*

dragons require is the purpose of an ongoing study led by Dr. Tim Jessop of the San Diego Zoo. Jessop has visited a number of Komodo dragon habitats to determine differences in the populations of dragons on different islands and their territory requirements, and to collect blood samples to create family trees based on the dragons' **DNA**. Since 1993, his team has tagged and examined nearly 300 Komodo dragons.

To closely study Komodo dragons, these giant lizards must first be trapped using what Jessop calls "a 10-foot (3 m) mousetrap" that is baited with goat meat. After a day or two, the rotting bait starts to stink—an irresistible lure for Komodo dragons. The bait is placed along a trail inside the trap, so as a hungry Komodo dragon eats the bait, he is forced to step all the way inside. The last piece of bait is attached to a device that slams the door shut when the dragon pulls on the meat.

The research is done quickly to minimize the stress put on the Komodo dragon. Researchers tie up the dragon's front and back legs with soft ropes and tape its snout closed so it cannot bite anyone. Then they look for a small electronic device called a passive integrated transponder (PIT) tag that may have been previously implanted just under the skin of the dragon's back leg. This device, which is about the size of a grain of rice, contains an identification number that is read using a handheld scanner—much like the scanners in a grocery store are used to read bar codes on products. If a dragon has previously been tagged, the number is recorded. If a dragon has no tag, one is implanted using a needle. The length and weight of the Komodo dragon is also measured and recorded, and a blood sample is taken for DNA analysis. Then the dragon is released, and the trap is baited again to continue the research on other dragons.

**Footprints resembling *Megalania prisca*'s found in Australia in 1979 led some people to suggest that this prehistoric lizard could still exist.**

**Komodo dragons are known to be strong swimmers, traveling between islands, and may dive to depths of 15 feet (4.6 m).**

Captive-breeding programs at zoos around the world are also aimed at better understanding Komodo dragons. There are about 60 Komodo dragons in U.S. zoos, many of which came from captive-breeding programs. At the Singapore Zoo in December 2009, a 16-inch (40.6 cm) hatchling was the first Komodo dragon born in an Asian zoo outside Indonesia—the sole success of a program that had spent 34 years trying to breed captive dragons. It is difficult to hatch dragons in zoos because of incompatible pairings of potential mates or because there are not enough females in captivity; also, little is known about the precise requirements for successful egg **incubation**. Scientists admit that successful hatchings—especially those resulting from parthenogenesis—are more a matter of luck than of a complete understanding of how Komodo dragons' bodies work.

Komodo dragons do not have to go the way of their dinosaur-era ancestors, though. Scientists, conservationists, and local people who understand the importance of Komodo dragons to the **ecosystem** in which they live are working to find a balance between the needs of Indonesian people and the needs of their national treasure, the Komodo dragon.

*In the water, a dragon tucks its hind feet close to its body and moves its tail back and forth to swim forward.*

# ANIMAL TALE: THE DRAGON'S BROTHER

**While the Komodo dragon is generally not considered to be a very attractive or friendly animal, it has exhibited intelligent and, at times, even playful behavior. This folk tale from Indonesia suggests that people should value the Komodo dragon despite its vicious reputation.**

On top of the highest mountain on Komodo Island lived a magical dragon-like being named Putri Naga, or Dragon Princess. She watched over the island and kept the mountain calm. One day, when a man named Najo was out hunting for deer, he strayed close to Putri Naga's mountain. As he looked up at Putri Naga above, her golden scales shimmered in the sun, and Najo believed she was the most beautiful creature he had ever seen.

Day after day, Najo begged Putri Naga to marry him, but she told him that she must remain in her mountain realm to keep the mountain calm. But Putri Naga had fallen in love with Najo, too. Finally, she agreed to marry him and left her mountain lair to join him in his village.

Putri Naga soon gave birth to twins. One was a human boy, whom she named Si Gerong, and one was a dragon girl, whom she named Orah. Najo was happy, and he felt proud of both of his beautiful children.

But the next day, the earth started to quake, and the highest mountain started to groan. Putri Naga had neglected the mountain for so long that it was no longer calm. It rumbled and spewed burning rock and smoke into the sky. Soon it covered the land with a smothering blanket of gray ash. The people ran to the sea and took to their boats. Animals fell to the ground, choking to death.

"I must return to the mountain," Putri Naga told Najo. Saddened, he understood that Putri Naga needed to calm the mountain to protect the island. "I would like to take our daughter with me," Putri Naga said. "You should keep our son." Najo agreed.

And so the human boy Si Gerong and dragon girl Orah never knew of each other. The boy grew up in the village, and the girl grew up in the forests of the highest mountain.

One day, when the twins had grown, Si Gerong went hunting in the forest. He followed a deer for some distance, unaware that he had strayed close to the mountain of Putri Naga. He raised his bow and shot the deer, but as he stepped forward to claim it, a large lizard appeared from the bushes and snatched up the deer.

Si Gerong raised his bow again to shoot the lizard. Just then, a beautiful creature appeared before him. She had shimmering gold scales and called him by name. It was Putri Naga.

"Si Gerong," she said, "my son." This shocked the boy, but he knew in his heart that she was his mother. "Do not harm the creature, for she is your sister, Orah."

At this, the lizard stood up and smiled at Si Gerong. He could see now that she was no ordinary lizard. "Take the deer, my sister," Si Gerong said. "And good health to you."

Orah smiled at her brother. "You are kind," she said. "Thank you."

And until recently, the villagers on Komodo Island fed the dragons of the forest to show respect and admiration for them, and the dragons did not harm the villagers, for they knew that the humans were their brothers.

## GLOSSARY

**camouflaged** – hidden, due to coloring or markings that blend in with a given environment

**captive-breeding** – bred and raised in a place from which escape is not possible

**carcass** – the dead body of an animal

**carrion** – the rotting flesh of an animal

**colonists** – people who establish settlements in a new land and exercise rule over the land from a distance

**DNA** – deoxyribonucleic acid; a substance found in every living thing that determines the species and individual characteristics of that thing

**ecosystem** – a community of organisms that live together in an environment

**egg tooth** – a hard, toothlike tip of a young bird's beak or a young reptile's mouth, used only for breaking through its egg

**evolved** – gradually developed into a new form

**extinct** – ended or died out completely

**herpetologist** – a person who studies reptiles and their lives

**incubation** – the process of keeping an egg warm and protected until it is time for it to hatch

**mammals** – warm-blooded animals that have a backbone and hair or fur, give birth to live young, and produce milk to feed their young

**metabolism** – the processes that keep a body alive, including making use of food for energy

**mythical** – relating to a collection of myths, or popular, traditional beliefs or stories that explain how something came to be or that are associated with a person or object

**nuisance** – something annoying or harmful to people or the land

**poaching** – hunting protected species of wild animals, even though doing so is against the law

**thermoregulate** – to keep the body's internal temperature within certain boundaries, regardless of the environmental temperature

### SELECTED BIBLIOGRAPHY

Braine, Tim. *The Jeff Corwin Experience: Asia: Land of the Komodo Dragon.* DVD. Silver Spring, Md.: Discovery Education, 2005.

Burden, W. Douglas. *Dragon Lizards of Komodo: An Expedition to the Lost World of the Dutch East Indies.* 1927. Reprint, Whitefish, Mont.: Kessinger Publishing, 2003.

De Lisle, Harold F. *The Natural History of Monitor Lizards.* Malabar, Fla.: Kreiger Publishing, 2006.

Molnar, Ralph E. *Dragons in the Dust: The Paleobiology of the Giant Monitor Lizard Megalania.* Bloomington: Indiana University Press, 2004.

National Geographic. "Animals: Komodo Dragon." National Geographic Society. http://animals.nationalgeographic.com/animals/reptiles/komodo-dragon.html.

Sprackland, Robert George. *Giant Lizards: The Definitive Guide to the Natural History, Care, and Breeding of Monitors, Iguanas, Tegus, and Other Large Lizards.* Kingston, Ont.: TFE Publishing, 2009.

*The average daytime temperature on Komodo Island is 80 °F (26.6 °C), allowing dragons to remain active year round.*

# INDEX

attacks on humans 21–22, 32, 34, 35
    and nuisance dragons 35
    peace offerings to prevent 34, 35

*Beowulf* 28, 29
    and traditional dragon imagery 28, 29

Burden, W. Douglas 30–32

cannibalism 22, 26, 30

conservation measures 38, 39–41
    research by Dr. Tim Jessop 40–41
    *see also under* zoos

cultural influences 12, 28, 29, 32, 34, 35, 38, 42
    dragon symbols in Asia 29
    film 32
    inspiration for *King Kong* 32
    on native Indonesians 12, 32, 34, 38, 42
    wildlife television shows 35

eggs 12, 18, 24, 25, 42
    guarding by females 25
    physical description 25
    and rainy season 25

hatchlings 22, 25–26, 42
    food sources 26
    growth rate 26
    life in trees 25–26
    physical characteristics 25
    predators 26

hunting 7–8, 12, 15–16, 22, 34
    ambushing technique 16
    feeding frenzy 16
    toxic bite 8, 15–16, 22

habitats 7–8, 11, 15, 30, 32, 34, 35, 37, 38, 39, 40, 44
    Indonesia 11, 34, 42, 44
    islands 7–8, 11, 15, 30, 32, 34, 35, 37, 38, 39, 40
        Flores 11, 39
        Gili Motang 11, 39
        Komodo 7–8, 11, 30, 32, 34, 35, 39, 44
        Rinca 11, 32, 39

Irwin, Steve 35

Komodo National Park 34, 35
    human population within 35

Kratt, Chris and Martin 35

life expectancy 22

mating 22, 24, 25, 42
    competition among males 24
    versus parthenogenesis 24, 42

movement 12, 16–17, 21, 42
    and metabolism 21

swimming 42
    and thermoregulation 21

nests 18, 24, 25
    in burrows 25
    raiding by other dragons 24

physical characteristics 12, 15, 16, 17, 18, 21, 26, 29, 30, 38, 41
    claws 18
    eyes 18
    feet 18, 38
    footprints 30
    forked tongue 12, 29
    gular pouch 17
    gums 16
    hearing 18
    Jacobson's organ 12
    legs 16, 41
    scales 15
    sight 21
    sizes 15, 26, 41
    teeth 15, 16

populations 38, 40

prey 7–8, 15, 16, 18, 21–22, 38
    birds 21
    carrion 15, 16
    sambar deer 15, 21
    small animals 21
    water buffalo 7–8, 15, 21

relatives 11–12, 29–30, 32, 37, 41, 42
    ancestors 11, 37, 41, 42
    beaded lizards 12
    monitor lizards 11–12, 29–30, 32, 37
        origin of "monitor" name 29–30

scientific research 11, 18, 30, 32, 40
    American Museum of Natural History 30, 32
    *see also* conservation measures

social behaviors 22

territories 22, 25, 38, 40

threats 38–39
    exotic animal collectors 38
    poaching 38
    urban expansion 38
    volcanic activity 38–39

Varanidae family 11

zoos 11, 18, 24, 26, 30, 32, 40, 42
    and captive-breeding programs 26, 42